I Like to Do That!

by Amy Moses
illustrated by Bill Colrus

Scott Foresman

Editorial Offices: Glenview, Illinois • New York, New York
Sales Offices: Reading, Massachusetts • Duluth, Georgia
Glenview, Illinois • Carrollton, Texas • Menlo Park, California

I like to dig like a 🐕.
dog

I like to hop like a 🐇.
rabbit

I like to sit like a .
kitten